If We Forget...

Wisdom and Reflections
from Those Living with Memory Loss

This edition published in 2012 exclusively for Oak Knoll Lutheran Church
and Lyngblomsten.

www.lyngblomsten.org
www.oklutheran.org

Printed by CreateSpace.

This book is dedicated to all persons with memory loss and all those who care for them.

A special thank you to The Gathering program participants for sharing and allowing others to get a sense of what is on their hearts and minds.

Why this Book

When looking at the terms Alzheimer's disease, memory loss, and dementia, there are many misunderstandings. Memory loss can affect different areas of the brain, and there are many types of memory loss—Alzheimer's disease is just one of them. Even while the brain is changing, the person experiencing memory loss still has areas of the brain very much intact. Following diagnosis, people with memory loss still want to be respected and allowed to utilize those intact brain areas to the greatest extent possible.

The Gathering is a program serving people with early- to mid-stage memory loss and giving respite to caregivers who desire a break. Under the leadership of Lyngblomsten in Saint Paul, Minnesota, the program is offered in collaborative partnerships with churches in the Twin Cities metro area. We learn a great deal from those with early memory loss, including what they are hoping for in programming to work their brains and keep them as healthy as possible for as long as possible.

Participants of The Gathering at Oak Knoll Lutheran Church (Minnetonka, MN) are courageous advocates and teachers for early memory loss work. This book compiles the voices of Oak Knoll The Gathering participants, sharing what they want others to know about people with memory loss. Their insightful comments illustrate how important it is to listen with our ears, hearts, and minds. **Let us use their words to help us better understand the world of those experiencing memory loss.**

Photos & Words

The photos in this book portray important people, places, and activities in the lives of The Gathering participants at Oak Knoll Lutheran Church. All photos are used with permission.

The comments recorded in this book are a combination of direct quotes and summarized conversations with participants of The Gathering at Oak Knoll Lutheran Church.

If We Forget...

PURPOSE

Hearing an Alzheimer's diagnosis was the biggest awakening of my life. I had always wanted to do good for others regardless of the endeavor, but I was never truly satisfied. As a result of my Alzheimer's disease diagnosis, my priorities changed. I found a new purpose for my life. Now my purpose in life is to do good *through* my disease. I want to make this disease worth having. I want to be an ambassador for others and their families who hear this diagnosis. I want to provide education to others about the disease and be an advocate for research and awareness at every level.

Knowledge

An early diagnosis of Alzheimer's is critical. Early treatment will allow us to have a better life for a longer time. Ultimately, we would not have to enter a care facility as soon. It is easier to have the diagnosis of Alzheimer's disease than worrying about whether you have it.

I want my pre-Alzheimer's friends to continue to be my friends. Remember the good times we've had together. Don't be afraid of being with me. Abandonment hurts. When a friend is diagnosed with Alzheimer's disease, contact them as soon as possible. Waiting too long makes the first contact much more difficult. Plan to go on this journey together. As a friend, you will learn to understand. Who knows? It could happen to any of us, and we would already have acquired wisdom through our friend.

Respect

Some things people say to us are well-intentioned, but we might find them hurtful. For example, *"I'm just like you—I forget things all the time too!"* or *"You don't look like you have Alzheimer's disease."* Instead, we like to hear you affirm us by letting us know that we are setting an example by accepting this disease with a positive, peaceful attitude.

Regardless of what stage of Alzheimer's I am in, treat me like you would want to be treated. Be understanding, caring, and mindful of my dignity and desires. I am a person first, who happens to have Alzheimer's.

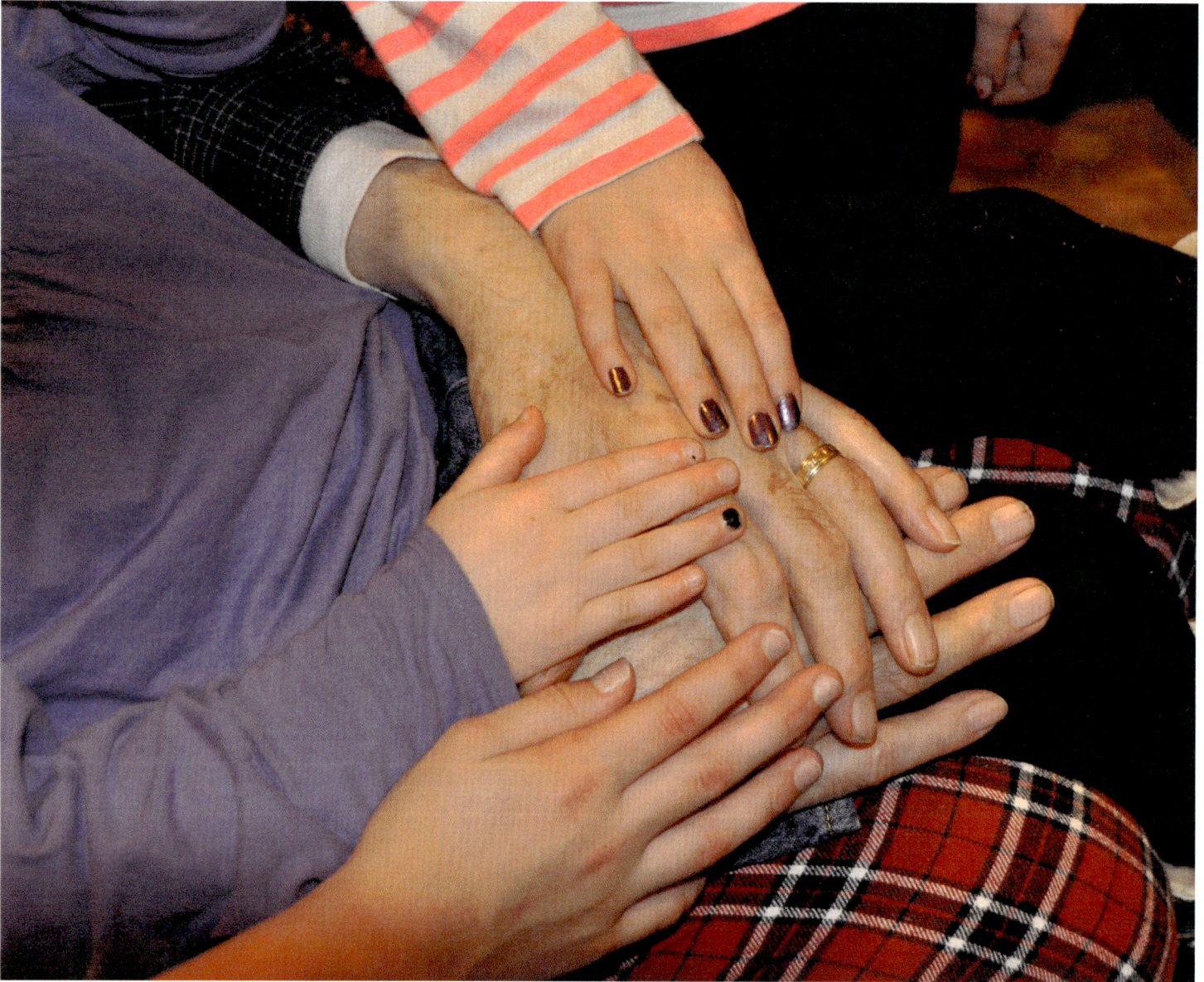

Children…just be with me. You make me happy when I can watch you play or when you just sit quietly with me.

Listen

Let me talk. You will sometimes need to be the patient listener. Correct me only when what I am saying changes the meaning of what I want to express. Assume that I understand what is being said even when I am unable to respond. Respect my intelligence. Include me in your conversations. Please don't talk around me as though I'm not there.

At times, I will need more time to process information. At those times, be patient and quiet because interruptions break my train of thought. I will also need additional time to form my responses.

PRESENCE

When I struggle to communicate, just sit with me. Communication can be silent. It's okay to put aside a conversation that has become frustrating.

Many conversations going on around me at the same time are distracting. I might become quiet in large group settings because the noise and multiple conversations cause me to develop information overload. I will let you know if I need a break from the group.

Let us attempt to do things independently if possible. We like your help and input, but we want to decide how to do things. We would prefer that you do not tell us how to do the task. We understand that you are trying to protect us from failure.

Individuality

Commands cause us to be defensive. It takes our voice
and freedom away. We will try to ask for help before
our care partners ask if we need assistance.
This helps us feel independent.

Together

We know we have Alzheimer's disease. We are
cognitive of many of the changes happening to us
even though we don't always understand the disease
medically. Respect us for what we are able to do.
Let's work as a team to decide what tasks need to be
done and determine how we can do them together.

With Alzheimer's we are learning to ask, *"Will you help me?"* Even more we are learning to ask, *"What can I do to help you?"* Men tend to be competitive. Asking for help feels like a loss of control. Alzheimer's is a great leveler. For friends and relatives who shy away from us because they don't know what to say or do, ask them to help in a specific way. It will break the ice, and they will feel needed.

My feelings for you
only grow stronger...
my trust in you
only becomes greater...
and my faith in our love
only becomes truer
with the beauty
of this wonderful season.

Happy Thanksgiving

Caregivers need the support of one another. Caregivers are happier when they can connect with others going through the same journey. They need to be healthy in order to function well as a caregiver. At the beginning, this journey can feel lonely for both the person with memory loss and for the care partner. Make that change by getting involved. Meet others. Form a new peer group and join a support group. Connect with the Alzheimer's Association.
Be a constant advocate for your needs.

DECISIONS

Having your driver's license taken away is horribly painful. When it's necessary, your care partner needs to <u>just do it</u>! There is no good way to take someone's driver's license. It impacts a person's freedom. We do not want to hurt ourselves or someone else by driving. We might get disoriented and lose our way. We will grieve and show our anger, but we will get through it.

Value the friendship of others who have Alzheimer's disease. It is important to find peers who understand. Learn from one another. Be there for one another.

How Philip the Firefly Saved Christmas

Santa called his little elves
To start packing the Sleigh.

It was snowing and blowing, and,.
It was time to go!

11

Kerchoooo sneezed Larry.

He looked so silly!
There he was with *Phillip the Firefly*
In a *Christmas ball* tied to his nose!

12

The Swampgoat

This kind of a night we knew the **SWAMPGOAT** was known
To roam.

ONCE IN A BLUE MOON when all was hidden by fog.
Where no light entered, no animal or human was out!
It was this kind of night
The horrid **SWAMPGOAT** would roam in search of prey.

14

We knew this. We saw the fog. We knew it was eerie.
When Peter went out that night we should have known.
Old beyond ages this fearsome creature lay underwater
in the murky swamp, seen only on this kind of night!

15

Share your stories while you are able. Talk about life, jobs, family and whatever is important to you. Write down or record your stories electronically. This is a gift for your family and friends. It might surprise you to discover what your stories reveal about yourself.

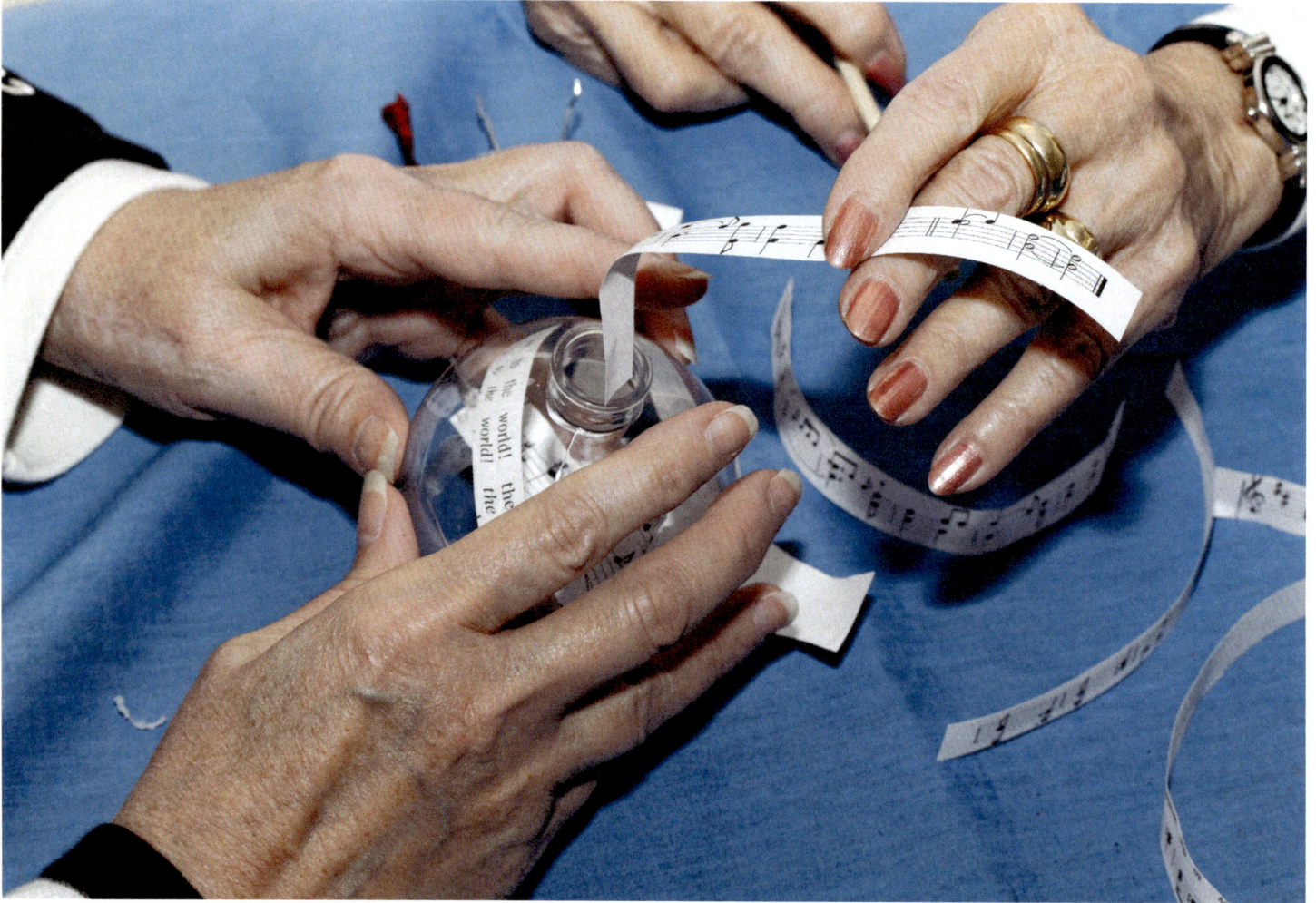

Do tasks that you can handle for as long as you can do them. Feel useful and helpful. For example, vacuuming and laundry are now part of my day. Contributing to household tasks are my way of being part of the team. My tasks are different now than what I did on my job, but they fulfill me. Do them joyfully.

Crosswords for every skill level!
Also available:
Crossword 200 PUZZLES
from The Nation's No. 1 Newspaper
Crossword
Crossword
Crossword 200 PUZZLES from The Nation's No. 1 Newspaper

Remember the best practices. Eat right, exercise daily and get stimulus socially, intellectually and creatively.

Help others. Volunteer while you can. Consider this the next stage of your life. Helping others makes life worthwhile. This is my new job!

As the Alzheimer's disease progresses, we understand that our abilities will change. Join us and support us on our journey into the unknown.

Future

Please understand that after diagnosis, we have time
to plan and live life to the fullest. Each day is a gift.
Is that any different from how anyone should strive
to live his or her life?

Acknowledgements:

To Linda Strand, Volunteer at The Gathering at Oak Knoll Lutheran Church,
for gathering and compiling all of the comments.

To Oak Knoll Lutheran Church for being in partnership with Lyngblomsten, and to lead volunteers and volunteers at Oak Knoll Lutheran Church for their commitment to The Gathering.

To all of The Gathering sites and volunteers around the metro.

To Lyngblomsten and the Lyngblomsten Foundation for sponsoring The Gathering partnership with local faith communities to provide this service.

To Lyngblomsten's The Gathering staff who believe in our purpose and work to have all of us dance together a beautiful waltz.

To Lyngblomsten's Marketing Communications team for their contributions of time and expertise to make this project a reality.

Cover: Design by Brett Stokke, member of Oak Knoll Lutheran Church
Images from iStockphoto

Photography: Dave Johnson, The Gathering lead volunteer
Pages 6, 28, 30, and 42
James Nash, Lyngblomsten volunteer
Pages 10, 16, 22, 34, 36, 38, 40, and 44

About The Gathering

The Gathering is part of Lyngblomsten's continuum of services to older adults. The program provides a day of cognitive and social stimulation for participants experiencing early- to mid-stage memory loss, and gives respite to caregivers who desire a break. The Gathering is staffed by a group of specially trained volunteers, and is offered in collaborative partnerships with churches who provide the facilities and host The Gathering.
Learn more at www.lyngblomsten.org/TheGathering.

Major funding for The Gathering is provided through grants and by the generosity of individuals who make financial gifts to the Lyngblomsten Foundation.
To make a donation to The Gathering, visit www.lyngblomsten.org/donate.

About Lyngblomsten

Lyngblomsten is a Christian nonprofit organization serving as a resource to older adults and their families by providing home- and community-based services, senior housing, and skilled nursing care. With a community of dedicated staff, volunteers, donors, and partner congregations, Lyngblomsten enhances the quality of life for older adults and those who care about them.

www.lyngblomsten.org | 1415 Almond Avenue, St. Paul, MN 55108 | (651) 646-2941